I0762723
KC BBQ
180

THE Little Book OF KC BBQ

ALSO BY JONATHAN BENDER

Cookies & Beer

Stock, Broth & Bowl

THE Little Book OF KC BBQ

★ A STORY OF SMOKE ★

JONATHAN BENDER

Andrews McMeel
PUBLISHING®

★ ★ ★

THIS BOOK IS DEDICATED TO THE FOLKS WHO WAKE UP
BEFORE THE SUN RISES TO TEND THE FIRES, ADJUST THE
DAMPERS, AND CHECK TEMPERATURES TO MAKE SURE
THE REST OF US HAVE SOMETHING DELICIOUS TO EAT.
IT'S DEDICATED TO KANSAS CITY, WHICH HAS WELCOMED ME
WITH OPEN ARMS AND BEEN A WONDERFUL PLACE TO DISCOVER
THE WORLD OF BARBECUE. AND, AS WITH ALL THINGS,
I DEDICATE THIS BOOK TO MY FAMILY, BECAUSE THEY ARE
THE PEOPLE I LOVE MOST IN THIS WORLD.

★ ★ ★

CONTENTS

INTRODUCTION

"Barbecue is like jazz. It can be as simple or complex as you want it to be."

BOB GIBSON

Kansas City is a barbecue town, forged in flames fed by hickory and oak wood for the past 150 years. It's how the world at large knows this Midwest city and the easiest way to fall into conversation with a local.

There is great joy in moving to Kansas City and discovering your favorite barbecue joint . . . until you discover that you might like the next place better. Brace yourself: Now you're in it. Suddenly, everyone has a spot you've got to try. Suddenly, you've got opinions. You find yourself recommending places to strangers. Yet you can't stop at simply naming a restaurant. Instead, you go on at length, whether the stranger wants an in-depth recommendation or not. You find yourself building your perfect plate with pulled pork from one place, burnt ends from a spot across town, and that one joint's sweet and smoky beans stippled with smoked bites of meat.

This is what it means to love barbecue in Kansas City. It is to debate it and revel in it and feel an intense pride for something that is uniquely ours. It is also to embrace the idea that KC is a barbecue melting pot, because Kansas City is where all meats come to be smoked. The city's central location made it a railroad hub with a booming stockyard district. An influx of Southern cooks like Henry Perry—the "Barbecue King" of Kansas City—meant that KC became willing to throw just about anything on a barbecue pit. Those brick-lined pits were fueled by oak and hickory; the hardwood trees are common to this region.

While the pitmasters of the early twentieth century built the legacy of Kansas City barbecue, the world of competition barbecue has led to a new generation of pitmasters and reinforced KC as a place synonymous with barbecue over the past thirty years. The American Royal World Series of Barbecue has crowned dozens of champions who have gone on to open restaurants, and the Kansas City Barbeque Society helped literally write the rules for how to judge barbecue.

For many people outside Kansas City, the style of barbecue here is defined by a thick barbecue sauce with a tomato and molasses base. This is the legacy of Rich Davis and KC Masterpiece, a sauce that rose to global prominence forty-five years ago. But here in Kansas City, folks will tell you to start your journey with burnt ends. The crispy edges of the brisket once given away as counter scraps are now revered for their exquisite combination of char and a tender beef center.

The Little Book of KC BBQ will teach you about the history of Kansas City barbecue along with how KC's approach differs from other regional barbecue in the United States. In order to understand KC barbecue, you also have to consider the traditions and flavor profiles of the other main regions—the Carolinas, Texas, and Memphis, Tennessee—regarded as fellow capitals of barbecue.

Be warned. Reading about barbecue will make you hungry. If you want someone else to do the cooking, there are drink pairing suggestions, alcoholic and nonalcoholic, for everything from chicken to brisket. And if you're looking for what to make for your next gathering or dinner, this book is packed with recipes from Kansas City chefs, pitmasters, and barbecue restaurants.

So grab a slab of ribs or a plate of burnt ends and discover all the ways that barbecue embodies the place and people of Kansas City.

BBQ, BARBECUE, BARBEQUE—WHAT'S THE DIFFERENCE?

Barbecue has always had many names. Before barbecue pits were built out of stones or bricks, Native Americans placed meat on elevated wooden frames atop smoldering fires. The Taíno people of the Caribbean called the stick frame a *barabicu,* which translates from the Arawak language to "wooden framework for supporting cooked or dried meat." The Hausa people of West Africa spoke of *babbake* when they roasted pork spiced with black pepper over an open fire.

Indigenous and African cooking methods were brought back to Europe in the sixteenth and seventeenth centuries. Spanish explorers referred to both the platform and the act of cooking as *barbacoa.* The French talked about *boucan,* and the English gave us the term "barbecue." The first recorded account of a barbecue is believed to be British author Edward Ward's *The Barbecue Feast; or the Three Pigs of Peckham, Broiled Under an Apple Tree*. The pamphlet, published in 1707, describes a community gathering where meat was cooked outside on a rack over an open flame.

We didn't stop at "barbecue" in the United States. The word has a host of phonetic spellings where the "*cue*" sound becomes "barbeque," "bar-b-q," or "BBQ." The dashes also mimic how we pronounce the word, with emphasis on each syllable. Sometimes it's capitalized like a proper noun or to give emphasis to the letters *b* and *q*, but if you're a grammarian seeking consistency, you won't find it here.

Need a governing body to back up your chosen spelling? The Kansas City Barbeque Society spells it with a *q*, while the North Carolina Barbecue Society opts for a *c*. This difference seems to stem from different historical spellings—specific to each region—of the art of barbecue (or barbeque).

If you're more practical, you might consider that the word was likely shortened for signs because it contained fewer letters. Fewer letters meant less space and a sign that cost less money to make. Pitmasters are often thrifty, figuring out how to do more with less. Barbecue restaurants weren't often fancy affairs. The earliest brick-and-mortar shops were often born out of roadside stands or outdoor pits. A casual spelling of "barbecue" was not only approachable but economical. Savings are important when you're a pitmaster who has to spend money on rent, employees, and the rising cost of meat. That said, pitmasters love to spin yarns and tales that romanticize a spur-of-the-moment decision to use "BBQ" instead of "barbeque." However you spell it, barbecue is delicious.

WHAT MAKES KC BBQ *Different?*

A TOUR OF REGIONAL BBQ STYLES

"Barbecue is the poetry of the South. It's its own art form."

MYRON MIXON

Barbecue means lots of different things to lots of different people. And your story of barbecue is often defined by where you grew up. The Carolinas, Texas, Memphis, and Kansas City all claim to be the headquarters of barbecue. Each barbecue capital has its own clear identity attached to the fuel they use, the spices that make up their rubs, and their feelings about sauce.

Barbecue is a menu shorthand for barbecued pork in the Carolinas, while thick slabs of beef brisket glisten on metal trays in Texas. Memphis has a long history of dry-rubbed ribs and a storied tradition of putting barbecue on everything from spaghetti to pizza. So, how does Kansas City barbecue differ from other prominent regions like Texas, Memphis, and the Carolinas?

TEXAS

Beef has been a central character in Texas barbecue for centuries. The plains of Texas were conducive to raising cattle, and large ranches meant plenty of beef was available for county celebrations and special occasions.

Cooking a rack of beef over an open pit was a way to feed lots of people and avoid waste in the days before refrigeration. Cowboys in West Texas would cook cuts of beef over live fire, mopping the meat with oil and vinegar, in a method that came to be known as "cowboy style."

German and Czech immigrants who settled in central Texas in towns like Fredericksburg discovered that smoking beef helped preserve the meat and yielded tasty results. Every story has a beginning, and Central Texas is the beginning of this one. Pitmasters there tend to use a simple dry rub—often just salt and pepper—generously applied to whole briskets. The meat (brisket, pork ribs, or sausage) is then smoked low and slow over mesquite, oak, or pecan wood. While there's typically white bread available on a platter or tray covered with butcher paper, you're on your own if you want a sandwich.

Beef ribs and pulled pork both get their due in East Texas, where meat is slowly cooked over hickory. African American cooks in East Texas swapped in brisket (which comes from the lower chest area of the cow) for the more traditional pork of the Southern states because it was less expensive. The tender meat, known for "falling off the bone," is often marinated with a tomato-based sauce, and barbecue joints will serve you up a sandwich of thick-cut brisket or roughly chopped pork, pickles, and hot sauce.

The most distinct aspect of barbecue in South Texas is that the barbecue sauce is sticky, sweet, and full bodied, because molasses is subbed in for the tomato of East Texas. A lot of menus feature cow tongue or head, rendered tender over long hours at low temperatures. South Texas barbecue is also known as barbacoa, a nod to the Mexican influences on its regional style.

Live-fire cooking takes center stage in West Texas, as meat is cooked over the direct heat of an open flame. That flame is fed mesquite wood, as the trees are abundant in the dry West Texas climate. Barbecue is done faster here, with shorter cook times at higher temperatures, meaning you won't have to wait long for the sausage or ribs cooked in an open pit.

MEMPHIS

Memphis doesn't shy away from big flavors. Pork shoulder and pork ribs are typically rubbed down with garlic, paprika, and pepper before being cooked in a big pit fueled by charcoal or hardwood coals. The sharp bite of that rub is often tamed by a tomato-based sauce that ranges from a deep orange to dark brown depending on how generous the cook is with molasses or tomato.

You'll find pulled pork sandwiches on practically every menu, where tender pork is buried beneath a healthy splash of barbecue sauce and a mountain of either tangy mustard-based coleslaw or a cool and sweet variety made with mayonnaise and sugar.

Ribs can be eaten dry, wet, or muddy. A dry rub is usually a mix of paprika and chili powder, while wet ribs are slathered in barbecue sauce. Muddy ribs split the difference and tend to get a combination of rub and sauce.

The city of Memphis has also been enshrined in barbecue lore because of the Memphis in May Championship Barbecue Cooking Contest. The annual competition, which began in 1978, attracts hundreds of teams and thousands of people in a city park along the Mississippi River. Competitive barbecue teams from across the country vie for more than a hundred thousand dollars in prize money over four days as part of the monthlong festivities, which also include a blues festival and running race.

In a nod to the importance of pork to Memphis barbecue, teams are judged on their skills cooking pork ribs, pork shoulder, and a whole hog. There's also a portion of the contest aimed at those new to working a grill or a smoker: the "Patio Porkers" competition, where amateur teams only have to enter pork ribs for judging in the hopes of besting professional and competitive pitmasters.

While pork is the festival's focus, teams can also enter what are known as "ancillary competitions," where they are judged on their hot wings, sauce, or "Anything But Pork" (beef, poultry, or even seafood).

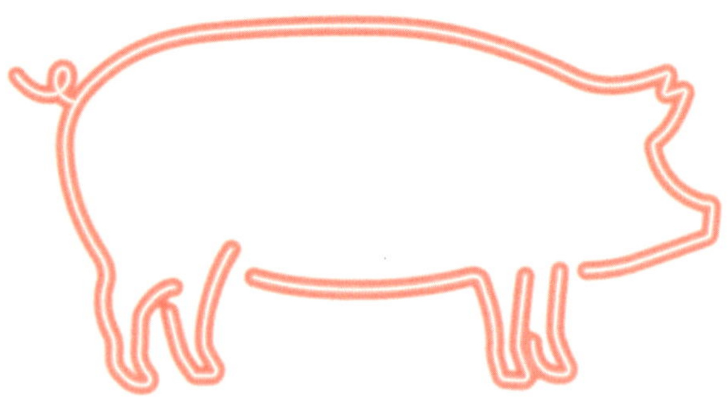

THE CAROLINAS

It's all pork in the Carolinas. Pulled pork. Chopped pork. Pork hash. Like something out of *Forrest Gump* but with pork instead of shrimp. North and South Carolina are both known for their barbecue, where the word “barbecue” on a menu is shorthand for barbecued pork.

In North Carolina, which the late author, chef, and television personality Anthony Bourdain anointed as the “cradle of barbecue,” they tackle pork differently in the eastern and western parts of the state. The original eastern style gets its distinct flavor from slow-smoked hogs over a bed of hardwood coals that are doused in a vinegar-and-pepper-based sauce. The pitmasters to the west add tomato to their sauce in a style known as “Lexington style” (named for the city where it was popularized) that riles up barbecue purists closer to the coast.

In South Carolina, which the state’s tourism department has deemed the “birthplace of barbecue,” pork is often served in the central part of the state with a mustard-based sauce made with brown sugar and vinegar. The rest of the state has a similar geographic split to North Carolina when it comes to barbecue sauce. The eastern portion of the state is committed to the punch of vinegar and pepper, while barbecue joints in the upstate regions and the western edges use a tomato base.

KANSAS CITY

While the other prominent regions focus on one kind of meat, Kansas City is a melting pot of barbecue. "If I had to use one word to describe Kansas City barbecue, that word is 'eclectic,'" says author and renowned barbecue judge Ardie A. Davis.

While the nation may know KC barbecue for its tomato-and-molasses-based sauce or burnt ends, the city has Southern influences and a willingness to cook everything from pork to beef to jackfruit. The early pitmasters of Kansas City served possum and woodchuck alongside brisket, and the same spirit applies today, even if the menu items have shifted to lamb ribs and pulled pork nachos.

Dry rubs in Kansas City are also complex affairs with a deep list of spices, herbs, and an occasional heaping scoop of brown sugar. The sweet or spicy notes then meld with the smooth smoke of hickory and oak. And then there's the thick sauce, laden with molasses and the slight acidity of tomato paste or ketchup, that leaves ribs sticky or adds depth to a plate of burnt ends.

The barbecue profiles of the Carolinas, Texas, Memphis, and Kansas City have literally been forged in fire over several centuries. Each new restaurant, food truck, or pit in the parking lot of a gas station must try to lure in customers either by offering a traditional take on barbecue or by playing against type by saucing ribs in Memphis or thick-slicing brisket in KC.

Barbecue will always be an edible slice of a place defined by the traditions of cooks as well as what's available to cook. And as pitmasters have tried to perfect a craft passed down over generations, they're also looking to cement their place in history by saying, "Our barbecue is better than your barbecue."

"Barbecue may not be the road to world peace, but it's a start."

ANTHONY BOURDAIN

THE *History* OF KC BBQ

Kansas City, Missouri, and barbecue are in a committed relationship, one that stretches back more than 150 years. In 1869, when it came time to celebrate the opening of the Hannibal Bridge—the first railroad crossing of the Missouri River—the city threw a barbecue. The bridge is central to this Midwestern barbecue tale because it connected the ranchers of the West with meat markets in the East, with Kansas City right in the middle.

The Kansas City Stock Yards were established two years after the bridge was completed, and the nearby West Bottoms neighborhood became a livestock hub. (The West Bottoms sits west of KC's downtown, with warehouses and former manufacturing buildings that come alive with vintage stores each weekend and haunted houses each fall.)

In time, millions of heads of cattle would travel through Kansas City annually. Bustling stockyards meant that KC had a steady supply of meat. But what were butchers and meatpackers to do with the less desirable parts (at the time) like ribs?

That's where pitmasters enter the picture. At the turn of the twentieth century, they took the tougher, cheaper cuts like brisket and ribs (where's the time machine, right?) and transformed them into something delicious with ingenuity and time. The most iconic pitmaster was Henry Perry.

Perry was the "Barbecue King," a Tennessee native who worked as a porter and cook on steamboats that traveled the Mississippi and Missouri Rivers. When he arrived in Kansas City in 1907, he quickly gained fame for his signature style of slow-cooking meat over hickory and oak, the drippings sizzling down onto the coals of his pit and luring in patrons with the tantalizing smell of smoked meat.

A story in *The Kansas City Star* from 1911 had a patron asking Perry, "What does a barbecue king have to do anyhow?"

His answer revealed his confidence and gift for self-promotion.

"He's got to barbecue any kind of meat better than anybody else, that's what he's got to do," replied Perry. "And I ain't lost my title yet."

Perry's reputation was built serving mutton, beef, pork, and woodchuck from a stand to workers in the Garment District. The downtown neighborhood (slightly east of where Quality Hill is located today and marked by a needle-and-thread sculpture at 8th and Broadway) was teeming with manufacturers, tailors, and seamstresses, producing more than 25 percent of the country's clothing a century ago. Perry routinely sold out of what he had cooked. His explanation for his success was deceptively simple.

"Cooking only over a fire made from hickory and oak woods, the meat gets that delicious flavor which is the cause of the tremendous popularity of barbecued meats," said Perry.

His barbecue, wrapped in newspaper, proved so popular that he decided to build out a spot in a burgeoning Black commercial district, what would become the 18th and Vine neighborhood—east of downtown Kansas City.

In 1911, Perry had a tent next to a brick-lined pit he built near the corner of 18th and Vine.

Before the end of the decade, he was able to open a brick-and-mortar restaurant—Perry's Barbecue—at 1514 E. 19th Street. His shop had windows laden with barbecue meats inside of a gleaming white brick building. Perry's Barbecue was in the heart of a busy neighborhood, close to the Paseo YMCA, Lincoln High School, and a bustling nightlife scene where jazz legends like Count Basie and Ella Fitzgerald would hold court into the early hours of the morning.

By the late 1920s, Perry was operating a location at 19th and Highland, selling his smoked meats and barbecue sauce. Around that time, there were close to one hundred barbecue spots in and around 18th and Vine. The district would eventually be known nationally for barbecue and jazz—spots like Dinty Moore Barbecue Meats, which served breakfast and chili in addition to smoked meats, and a space at 1403 E. 17th Street, originally run by Perry and then by Charles Bryant, that offered "barbecue meats and hot sauce" for "other barbecue stands, drugstores, and picnics."

The lore of Perry's barbecue spread to other towns—his name and food would be praised by fans in the papers of Topeka, Kansas, and Milwaukee, Wisconsin. And the developing national reputation of Kansas City as a barbecue town led to fierce competition. As pitmasters surveyed the barbecue landscape, they realized they'd have to offer something different to stand out. Pitmasters like Jack Fiorella—his father, Russ, started the original Jack Stack in 1957—added steak, seafood, and lamb ribs to a barbecue lineup slow-cooked over hickory. Fiorella's Jack Stack also added a cheesy corn bake (a bubbly crock of melted cheese and corn studded with bits of hickory-smoked ham) to its offering of sides, expanding beyond the traditional offerings of barbecue beans and slaw.

The legend of Kansas City's barbecue restaurants also spread outside of the city thanks to radio broadcasters and food writers. The announcers at Municipal Stadium, the former home of the Kansas City Royals and Kansas City Monarchs, would talk about the smells of smoked meat wafting from the 18th and Vine District. Travelers to Kansas City flocked to Arthur Bryant's Barbecue on 18th and Brooklyn after Calvin Trillin, the acclaimed food writer, declared it "the best damn restaurant in the world" in a 1974 *New Yorker* essay.

The 1980s may have cemented Kansas City as a barbecue town in the eyes of the rest of the country. Rich Davis's KC Masterpiece became a fixture on grocery store shelves nationwide. The flavors of tomato and molasses—the idea that Kansas City was a sauce town (a notion that many native Kansas Citians might disagree with)—became part of the script when discussing KC barbecue. In the same decade, the American Royal World Series of Barbecue was launched and the Kansas City Barbeque Society was founded. Competitive barbecue teams made the annual pilgrimage to Kansas City seeking glory at the former, and competitions were held around the globe with rules that originated in Kansas City thanks to the latter.

The barbecue restaurant landscape in Kansas City has been defined by pitmasters from the competition circuit over the past thirty years. Joe's Kansas City Bar-B-Que, originally Oklahoma

Joe's, opened in 1996 after years of competing and catering. Their success demonstrated the path for dozens of pitmasters, who also continued to spread the legend of Kansas City barbecue by selling award-winning rubs and sauces to stores and would-be grill masters across the country.

KC became a place to test your barbecue mettle. Your barbecue had to be good because of the long tradition of cooking but also because of the sheer number of joints, which tends to fluctuate right around one hundred different restaurants. If you could succeed in the crowded field of pitmasters here, you would know that your barbecue was a worthy successor to the "Barbecue King."

A LITTLE *Competition* GOES A LONG WAY

"No barbecue is worth anything unless it takes all day."

WILLIAM FAULKNER

Barbecue is sometimes a good excuse to argue and a great way to earn bragging rights. Kansas City's barbecue identity has been forged in the flames of competition barbecue.

Kansas City is home to the American Royal World Series of Barbecue and the Kansas City Barbecue Society. The former is the largest barbecue competition in the world, attracting hundreds of teams annually who come to Kansas City, Kansas, to try to claim their place among the very best. The latter is the sanctioning body that certifies barbecue judges and helps organizations put on hundreds of contests across the globe.

WELCOME TO THE SHOW

Kansas City's barbecue legacy has been tied to the stockyards since the late 1800s. While pitmasters were sourcing unwanted cuts like ribs, the American Royal—a nonprofit agricultural organization—was putting on livestock shows.

The first show was the National Hereford Exhibition at the Kansas City Stockyards in 1899, where more than three hundred head of cattle representing "60 different herds from all over the country" were sold at auction, in front of a crowd of more than fifty thousand people.

The American Royal adopted its current name in 1902, a nod to the British Royal Agricultural Fair. Over the next decade, shows dedicated to horses and dairy cows joined the lineup. "The Royal," as it's known colloquially, centered itself around education. It taught kids about our food system and agriculture. Students often judged livestock competitions. In 1928, a group of thirty-three students visiting KC to judge an American Royal show formed the Future Farmers of America.

The American Royal continued to branch out. It added an annual rodeo in 1949, and in 1980, the first American Royal World Series of Barbecue was held in the West Bottoms neighborhood (at the site of the former Kansas City Stockyards). It was there that a doctor named Rich Davis had his barbecue sauce—soon to be renamed KC Masterpiece—deemed the best sauce on the planet. The annual contest grew into the largest barbecue competition in the world.

In 2015, the barbecue competition was held in the parking lots surrounding Arrowhead Stadium—home of the Kansas City Chiefs—before it moved the following year to the Kansas Speedway. Hundreds of teams show up each year on the infield in the hopes of hearing their name called as the Grand Champion. Only one will sit on a literal throne to receive a novelty check and, perhaps more importantly, bragging rights.

WHAT'S A COMPETITION WITHOUT RULES?

When the Kansas City Barbeque Society (KCBS) launched in 1985, founders Rich Welch and Gary and Carolyn Wells pledged that the "only requirement for membership was that none of it be taken seriously." KCBS was started as a lighthearted group to compete in local barbecue contests. It's grown to be so much more over four decades. Today, KCBS sanctions hundreds of contests, trains certified barbecue judges, and has more than ten thousand members.

Barbecue competitions, like golf tournaments, are multiday affairs. Teams will usually start cooking on a Friday or Saturday night to turn in their barbecue for judging on the following afternoon. KCBS recognizes four official categories: chicken, pork ribs, pork shoulder, and beef brisket. But contests often have additional prizes for the best side, appetizer, or dessert.

The key piece of a KCBS contest is that the judging is done blind by certified judges. KCBS offers classes—you have to be at least sixteen years old to attend—to teach their judges how to taste and rate barbecue. The judges score the entries based on flavor, presentation, and tenderness. Each judge also takes the following oath, administered for years by cookbook author, barbecue maven, and Kansas City native Ardie A. Davis:

> *I do solemnly swear to objectively and subjectively evaluate each barbecue meat that is presented to my eyes, my nose, my hands, and my palate. I accept my duty to be an official KCBS Certified Judge, so that truth, justice, excellence in barbecue, and the American way of life may be strengthened and preserved forever.*

Success in competitions has led to a new vanguard of barbecue restaurants in Kansas City, giving pitmasters the chance to turn catering jobs into brick-and-mortar establishments. The most well-known might be Joe's Kansas City Bar-B-Que—the barbecue joint was started in a gas station in 1996 by Jeff and Joy Stehney with their then-partner Joe Don Davidson (the Joe in Oklahoma Joe's, the restaurant's original name).

Over the past thirty years, Kansas City's barbecue scene has been impacted by competition cooks like the late Rob Magee of Q39, where they finish their brisket on a wood-fired grill. Or Mike and Joe Pearce of Slap's BBQ in Kansas City, Kansas, who choose to cook their brisket hot and fast (at a high temperature for a short period of time) rather than the traditional low-and-slow method (low temperature for a long time) on a smoker. Or Todd Johns of Plowboys Barbeque, who sells thousands of pounds of rub each year to aspiring pitmasters hoping that the next competition is the one that launches their barbecue into the conversation.

TO GRILL OR TO *Smoke?* THAT IS THE QUESTION

"Barbecue is eternal. It's like the Mississippi River; it's big and it's simple and it takes its own sweet time."

C. B. STUBBLEFIELD

GRILLING, BARBECUING, AND SMOKING—WHAT'S THE DIFFERENCE?

The words "barbecue" and "grill" get jumbled together all the time. You go to a barbecue where someone is grilling. But you go to eat barbecue at a restaurant, where the brisket for your sandwich was cooked in a smoker. So, what's the difference?

GRILLING is cooking meat or vegetables for a short period of time at a high temperature. You typically grill hot dogs or steaks on a grate that sits directly over a flame.

BARBECUING is cooking large cuts of meat, like pork shoulders or beef brisket, over indirect heat where the meat is not immediately above the flames. You can crank the temperature to cook something hot and fast or make it an all-day affair and cook your ribs low and slow.

SMOKING is cooking over indirect heat with the added element of smoke. Slow-burning wood adds the aroma and flavor of smoke to the meat. The smoke comes from burning wood logs, chips, or pellets that also help form the bark—the crispy outer layer—on a pork butt.

WHAT TYPE OF WOOD SHOULD YOU USE WHEN YOU SMOKE?

Wood is how you instill the flavor of a place into barbecue because wood is directly impacted by the climate where the trees have been harvested. The amount of precipitation and the composition of the soil make a huge difference once you add heat to that wood and get smoke.

The main types of wood used for barbecue in the United States are hardwoods, nut woods, and fruit woods that have been cured or dried. Hardwoods are popular choices because mesquite, hickory, or oak is abundant and creates enough smoke to penetrate thicker cuts like brisket. Nut woods, like pecan or walnut, offer a nutty flavor or slightly sweet notes to pork or chicken. Pitmasters use milder fruit woods like apple, cherry, peach, and pear for smoking poultry, fish, and pork. Those fruit woods often have a lighter, slightly sweet smoke.

In Kansas City, hickory and oak are used. The two hardwoods are reasonably priced and readily available. Hickory and oak are also sturdy enough to stand up to the meatiness of beef without overpowering tender pork. Mesquite provides the strongest smoke flavor, one that can be delicious in moderation, for thick cuts like beef ribs.

LOGS. An outdoor pit is typically flanked by stacks of wood waiting to fuel tomorrow's lunch. The wood is stacked to dry or cure, so it's handy when you need to grab a stick or two. Logs are larger and are typically used with a fire that's burning hotter—think 275 degrees instead of 225 degrees—to turn the logs into embers, which provide heat and clean smoke that is flavorful without being bitter.

CHIPS. Wood chips are, you guessed it, wood that has been put through a wood chipper. The smaller pieces of wood are about the size of a quarter. Chips burn quickly, and a handful might last a little over an hour when you're cooking. Chips can be used with a grill to add smoke as a finishing touch to vegetables or burgers.

CHUNKS. *The Goonies* isn't the only place you'll find Chunk. In this case, chunks are chopped pieces of wood that range in size from a Ping-Pong ball to a peach. Chunks don't burn as quickly as chips because they're larger and denser. Many backyard cooks add a chunk or two at the start of a cook. Chunks are a good source of slow and steady smoke. A few chunks are usually enough for a rack of ribs and some brisket.

PELLETS. Pellets are small bits of compressed, wet sawdust. The sawdust, typically made of oak, is pressed into long rods, roughly the thickness of a pencil, and then cut down into small bits about the size of an eraser. Fans will tell you they burn hot and clean, providing consistent heat because they're uniform in size.

CHARCOAL IS WOOD TOO

Lump charcoal is made from chunks of wood that have been burned. The dried chunks burn hotter and produce less ash than charcoal briquettes, which burn longer and at a more consistent temperature.

Charcoal briquettes—compressed bits of wood shaped into little bricks—became popular a century ago when Henry Ford needed to figure out what to do with all the sawdust and wood scraps that were produced by his automobile plants in Detroit, Michigan. Ford had a pair of partners in that early venture: Thomas Edison and Edward G. Kingsford.

★ DID YOU KNOW? ★

DON'T BE A SAP

Pine trees smell amazing during the holidays or in the crisp, clean air of winter. But coniferous trees like pine or spruce are not great choices for smoking. The sap inside can add unwanted flavors to your next dinner masterpiece.

"It has long been acknowledged that the single best restaurant in the world is Arthur Bryant's Barbeque at 18th and Brooklyn in Kansas City."

CALVIN TRILLIN

Hot DISH:

BURNT ENDS

Kansas City pitmasters are willing to cook a lot of different meats. And the idea is that they've taken the time to understand how to do each one right. (Here's a hint: It's almost always low and slow.) But Kansas City isn't just an aggregator of barbecue; we're also innovators. The world can thank us for one very key barbecue menu item: burnt ends.

Burnt ends are the crispy, fatty ends of the brisket. The part that has a little bit of char, called "bark," and a whole heap of flavor. They're crunchy on the outside and then luscious and meaty on the inside. These pieces of barbecue gold were once given away for free. They were the scraps, the bits that were too charred and crunchy for sandwiches. More often than not, they were snacks for the cooks or discarded or tucked away inside a pot of boiling beans.

Burnt ends may very well have been a tragic story, a piece of delicious culinary achievement forgotten to time. But Arthur Bryant, the late namesake of the restaurant down on Brooklyn Avenue, was friends with writer Calvin Trillin. It was a friendship forged by smoke and one that would change the arc of barbecue in Kansas City and the world.

Trillin, a longtime writer for *The New Yorker* magazine, penned a pivotal article in 1972 for *Playboy*. In the face of a particularly disappointing meal, Trillin lamented that someone in Kansas City was right now receiving the "burned edges" of a brisket for free. Perhaps it's appropriate that something so decadent and indulgent was revealed to the world in the pages of *Playboy*.

Those charred bits—the scraps—that folks grabbed off the counter while they were waiting in line suddenly took center stage. That smoky goodness captured the imagination of Kansas City eaters. This is how the myth of burnt ends was born, and the spice, fat, and incredible texture of these tiny barbecue morsels is why they're still so popular five decades later.

Burnt ends didn't always have a name or a slot on the menu. They were "crispies" and "brownies" and small charred bits that were a free taste for customers. But just like mice and cookies, once folks had a taste of those crispy, fatty morsels, they wanted more.

Pitmasters are perhaps Kansas City's most resourceful and enterprising businesspeople. As customers began asking for burnt ends, even if they didn't yet have a name, pitmasters were only too happy to sell them piles of the scraps. Waste not if you can eke out a little profit.

Over a period of years, burnt ends went from an informal snack not fit for the slicer to a bona fide menu item. However, there was one big problem. The demand—our insatiable hunger for the smoke and spice and rich flavor—far outstripped the supply. Briskets naturally taper at the edges, and those charred bits, chopped from the edges, were only enough for a few plates at a time. Barbecue customers felt the pain of Oliver Twist all too quickly.

But pitmasters, over time and through trial and error, found a way to replicate what happens to the tapered edges and use more of the brisket. If you're wondering where the brisket is on a cow, it's located on the lower chest below the shoulder and above the leg.

A whole brisket has two parts: the point and the flat. The larger flat is often sliced and used for sandwiches. It's the leaner part of the brisket. The fattier point, when treated right, develops a nice, crusty exterior (known as the bark) and a tender, juicy interior (a result of the fat rendering during the meat's extended stay in the smoker).

Burnt ends are no longer made one way. Today, you may get burnt ends from the edges, or you may get chopped up pieces of point or flat. After chopping or cubing the brisket to make the pieces that we call burnt ends, pitmasters may either try to hide mistakes with sauce or consider the sauce the cherry on this particular meat sundae.

Burnt ends are KC's unique contribution to the barbecue landscape. Just as pulled pork snuck onto menus in the metro, burnt ends are starting to pop up in other barbecue regions across the country. The legend of burnt ends is still being written, but the origin is clear. This is Kansas City, the home of burnt ends.

"Barbecue is a dance of flavors, a symphony of smoke and spice."

JOHNNY TRIGG

HERE'S THE RUB: KANSAS CITY *Style*

Most barbecue rubs start with a combination of salt, sugar, and pepper. Then folks—outside of Texas, where a rub might start and end with salt and pepper—add in savory or spicy elements to complement the meat. Kansas City's style of rub is distinct from the salt and pepper of Texas, the onion and garlic of Memphis rubs, and the paprika pop often found in the Carolinas.

KC's barbecue sauce pours thick with the body and sweetness of molasses, but before the sauce is added, meat will be rubbed with a blend of spices that's salty, sweet, and a touch spicy. Kansas City–style barbecue rubs tend to spin every aspect of the flavor wheel delicately, offering little moments of heat or sweet—like the crackling of Pop Rocks—without ever going too far in one direction.

The balance of salt, pepper, and brown sugar is often accentuated with notes of dehydrated garlic and onion or little hints of smoke. It's the spice choices or small additions to a balanced base that create flavor memories for fans of KC's legacy barbecue joints. Jack Stack's KC Meat & Poultry Rub gets a subtle note from a touch of hickory smoke. Arthur Bryant's Meat & Rib Rub also uses hickory smoke but has a light citrus note thanks to orange juice concentrate. Gates's Original Classic Rub has the distinct background of celery seed (a common, but not widely known, ingredient found in many Kansas City barbecue sauces).

RUB IS A FLAVOR BUILDING BLOCK

Rub is applied before meat is placed in the smoker or on the grill. While there are lots of rubs on store shelves, seasoned pitmasters and grill jockeys develop their own recipes over time, tweaking the heat or sweet levels to their own taste.

Despite the name, rub isn't always rubbed in: It's often sprinkled atop meat. Rub adds flavor to meat and helps form a crust (the bark) that seals in the juices. Dry rubs are made with spices and herbs, while wet rubs are those same spices and herbs mixed with oil or water.

WHERE THERE'S BARK, YOU SHOULD BITE

Bark is the crispy, flavorful outer layer—like Earth's crust—that forms on the outside of a brisket when it's smoked. Sugars caramelize. Fat renders. And as the spices dissolve into the rendered fat, a glaze begins to form on the outside of the meat.

Over time, the spices dry out and form a light crust. After several hours, you'll open the smoker door to see delicious bark with a whiff of smoke. The bark helps seal all the juices inside for a crispy bite on the edges that surrounds tender meat.

★ DID YOU KNOW? ★

BLOOMING ISN'T JUST FOR ONIONS

Want big flavors? Try blooming your spices. Warm a pan or skillet over medium heat. Add your dry spices, like cumin or black pepper, and shake the pan often. If the spices stay in direct contact with the heat too long, they'll burn.

In only a minute or two, you'll smell the oils being released by your spices. That's how you know they're done. Take them off the heat and let them cool. Or add oil—at a rough ratio of one part oil to two parts dry ingredients by weight—to form a paste. Cook for another minute on low to let the spices and oil blend to create a wet rub.

"If you don't got no sauce, then you're lost. But you can also get lost in the sauce."

GUCCI MANE

A TRUE MASTERPIECE:

SAUCE

KANSAS CITY'S BARBECUE MASTERPIECE

KC Masterpiece, arguably the world's most famous barbecue sauce, started in Kansas City. Child psychiatrist Rich Davis was an enthusiastic home cook with a penchant for making his own sauce.

In 1978, his sauce was known as "K.C. Soul Style Barbecue Sauce," and he delivered it to stores in the back of his station wagon. Just two years later, his sauce was named the "Best Sauce at the Planet" at the inaugural American Royal World Series of Barbecue.

The sauce was slightly sweeter than most table sauces in Kansas City at the time. Arthur Bryant's sauce was a punch of vinegar and pepper while Gates Bar-B-Q offered a sauce that was a blend of tomato, vinegar, and sugar.

Davis's original barbecue sauce got its body from molasses and ketchup. The sweetness of the molasses was balanced by the acidity of vinegar and a bit of liquid smoke. It was renamed to "KC

Masterpiece" after Davis—an accomplished jazz pianist—had declared that it was his masterpiece.

KC Masterpiece took off, and less than a decade after its launch, Davis's condiment company was purchased by the Kingsford Products Company, a division of Clorox. Kingsford introduced KC Masterpiece to the nation, solidifying Kansas City as the home of tomato-and-molasses-based barbecue sauce. Children of the 1990s likely remember that KC Masterpiece was the barbecue flavor for Lay's potato chips for a number of years.

Davis retained the rights to use his sauce and the name "KC Masterpiece" for restaurants, opening locations in the Kansas City metro area, St. Louis, and Chicago. The KC Masterpiece barbecue restaurants operated for more than two decades, with the original location in Overland Park being the last to close in 2009.

After a long career as a psychiatrist, entrepreneur, and national barbecue expert, Davis died at the age of 89 in 2015. But the sauce he created is on shelves across the world, forever linking the words "Kansas City" and "barbecue."

MUSCHUP: THE FORGOTTEN CONDIMENT MASH-UP

Barbecue sauce wasn't the only idea that caught the attention of Rich Davis. He was also trying to market a new condiment alongside KC Masterpiece. He had big dreams for Muschup (a ketchup-mustard mash-up) and Dilled Muschup (relish, ketchup, and mustard). The idea of one hot dog topping in a single bottle didn't really catch on, and Davis wisely leaned into barbecue sauce.

THE LEGEND OF *Fire* SAUCE

"Barbecue sauce."

TED LASSO

n the beginning, there was fire sauce. We're talking face-melting sauce. Barbecue sauce that didn't just challenge you; it taunted you.

The story of fire sauce begins, as do all things in Kansas City barbecue, with Henry Perry. The Tennessee import, who perfected his craft cooking on steamships up and down the Mississippi River, arrived in KC at the turn of the twentieth century as part of the Great Migration.

The "Barbecue King" built a following around his penchant for pit-smoking beef and possum over hickory and oak. He then slathered that slow-cooked meat in an eye-stinging baste of pepper and vinegar as a nod to his Tennessee roots.

> [PERRY] USED TO ENJOY WATCHING HIS CUSTOMERS TAKE THEIR FIRST BITE OF A SAUCE THAT HE MADE TOO HOT FOR ANY HUMAN BEING TO EAT WITHOUT EIGHT OR TEN YEARS OF WORKING UP TO IT.
>
> CALVIN TRILLIN

THE HEIRS TO THE BARBECUE KING

Henry Perry had a restaurant managed by Charlie Bryant, a young man from Texas with a brother named Arthur. When Perry passed in 1940, he left that restaurant to Charlie. When Charlie retired, Arthur stepped in and decided to remake Perry's sauce in the barbecue joint that has become a staple in the city's 18th and Vine District.

The vinegar stayed, as did the pepper, but the heat was toned down significantly. Today, Arthur Bryant's is one of the two barbecue sauce poles in Kansas City. It has a vinegar base with punchy notes of curry powder, tomato, paprika, and drippings from the meat. The other is Gates Bar-B-Q.

THE CONTENDER FOR THE THRONE

Gates also traces its lineage back to Perry. George and Arzelia Gates bought Ol' Kentuck Bar-B-Q at 19th and Vine in 1946, the same year that Arthur Bryant took over for his brother, Charlie.

The pitmaster at Ol' Kentuck was named Arthur Pinkard, and he had learned to cook from Henry Perry. Pinkard, in turn, taught George and his son, Ollie, how to run the pits. Ol' Kentuck became Gates & Son's Bar-B-Q.

The sauce, which is still true to the original recipe, is a blend of tomato, vinegar, onion, and garlic powder. It's got a bit more roundness and sweetness than its vinegar-forward competitor at Bryant's.

"Good people drink good beer."

HUNTER S. THOMPSON

Barbecue will always be the star of the show, but you can elevate a backyard get-together or a plate of smoked meat with the right drink pairing.

There's a reason that iced tea and lemonade are staples on barbecue menus or picnic tables. But your bar doesn't have to stop with an Arnold Palmer (half lemonade, half iced tea) and beer. You can surprise your guests and yourself with unexpected combinations.

Take the same approach that you might take to pairing wine and chocolate or cookies and beer (seriously, try a milk stout with an Oreo) and look for complementary or contrasting flavors in what you're drinking and eating. The right pair brings out hidden notes in both parts of your meal, with each sip bringing something surprising.

BOOZY PAIRINGS

Cocktail menus are becoming a trend at barbecue restaurants. Here's what to order (or serve) the next time you're looking for a libation to accompany your barbecue.

BRISKET & LAMBRUSCO. The semi-sparkling Italian red wine is a refreshing companion to fatty brisket. A little bit of bubbles does a lot of work here. You can also try Lambrusco with smoked beef sausage.

PULLED PORK & BOURBON. Rich pork is well met by the slightly sweet notes in bourbon. You might get a little vanilla, caramel, or even oak that can play off smoke nicely. Bourbon over ice works, or you can make a bourbon apple cider smash with bourbon, apple cider, honey, and lemon juice.

PORK RIBS & ROSÉ. Rosé is a terrific complement to pork ribs. Opt for a light, fruity wine to let the pork ribs shine without overwhelming the delicate flavors that took hours to build in a smoker.

BEEF RIBS & PALE ALE. The medium-bodied brew has enough legs to stand up to the deep smoke of beef ribs. The malt and mild hop bitterness work in concert with the fat and flavor of a saucy or dry-rubbed rib.

BARBECUE CHICKEN & PIMM'S. This gin-based liqueur is bursting with herbs, warm spices, and caramelized orange flavors that sing with a plate of barbecue chicken, as well as back notes of honey that are terrific with sweet or spicy barbecue sauce. And Pimm's blends beautifully with lemonade or ginger beer for a simple cocktail pairing.

NONALCOHOLIC PAIRINGS

There are lots of fun ways to play around with carbonation and offer another option alongside iced tea and lemonade.

BRISKET & STRAWBERRY SODA. Sweet meets smoke. The char from the bark on brisket—particularly burnt ends, if you can get them—is elevated by the bold punch of strawberry.

PULLED PORK & SPARKLING CIDER. Much like the bubbles from Lambrusco, the fizzy drink brings a sweet note that can match the brown sugar in many barbecue sauces. A bit of tartness and acidity match the pork well too.

PORK RIBS & PEACH SPARKLING WATER. The bubbly water brings a bit of fruit to the party that picks up the natural sweetness in pork ribs. You could also opt for unflavored sparkling water, as the bubbles are a nice palate cleanser.

BEEF RIBS & DR PEPPER. The slightly spicy soda is often used as a rib or brisket marinade. The cherry notes in Dr Pepper are brilliant with beef ribs, with the sweetness of the soda melding well with the smoke infused in the rib meat.

BARBECUE & WATERMELON AGUA FRESCA. This is a summer vibe. You get some spice and sweetness from the chicken and refreshment with each sip.

To make two servings of watermelon agua fresca, place 2 cups cold water, 2 cups cubed watermelon, 2 tablespoons sugar, and 1 tablespoon lime juice in a blender. Blend until smooth. Pour the mixture into a pitcher through a strainer to remove the solids. Chill the agua fresca in the fridge for thirty minutes. Serve over ice.

RECIPES

Barbecue is a great place for innovation and experimentation. Whether you want to add a little smoke to your brunch cocktail or create ribs that stick in your imagination, here's a set of lip-smacking barbecue recipes.

APPETIZERS AND SIDES

BBQ MEATBALLS

ARTHUR BRYANT'S BARBEQUE

MAKES 36 TO 42

There's a reason you're excited for a tray of meatballs at a party. Use a toothpick to skewer these savory bites or load up a Hawaiian roll for a perfect accompaniment to watching football.

1½ pounds ground beef (80/20)
½ pound ground pork
½ cup breadcrumbs
2 eggs
¼ cup whole milk
2 tablespoons Arthur Bryant's Meat & Rib Rub*
½ cup finely chopped yellow onion
2 cloves garlic, minced
2 tablespoons chopped parsley (optional)
1 cup Arthur Bryant's Original BBQ Sauce*

**If you don't have Arthur Bryant's rub or sauce, look for a rub that balances the sweetness of brown sugar with smoke and paprika and a sauce that has a tart base of tomato and vinegar.*

1. Preheat the oven to 375°F. Line a baking sheet with parchment paper or lightly grease it with butter.
2. In a large mixing bowl, combine the ground beef, ground pork, breadcrumbs, eggs, milk, rub, onion, garlic, and parsley, if using. Mix gently until combined. Do not overmix to avoid dense meatballs.
3. Roll the meat mixture into 1½-inch meatballs. Place the meatballs on the baking sheet in even rows so that they aren't touching, about ½ inch apart.
4. Bake the meatballs in the oven for 20 to 25 minutes, until cooked through with an internal temperature of 165°F.
5. Remove the meatballs from the oven. Brush them generously with barbecue sauce. Place the baking sheet back in the oven for 5 minutes to allow the sauce to caramelize. Remove the meatballs and serve immediately.

CHEESY CORN BAKE

JACK STACK BARBECUE

SERVES 10 TO 12

Cheesy with a bit of smoke, this popular side from Jack Stack Barbecue is year-round comfort food. The slight sweetness of corn and rich cheese base are great partners for the pepper and char on ribs or smoked meats. It's an unconventional barbecue side—a cheesy option that doesn't involve macaroni—that has become one of the hallmarks of Jack Stack. This is the recipe that folks will ask you to bring to the picnic.

2 tablespoons unsalted butter
4 tablespoons all-purpose flour
⅛ teaspoon garlic powder
¾ cup whole milk
3 ounces cream cheese, cut into 1-inch cubes
6 ounces sharp cheddar cheese sauce
3 (10-ounce) packages frozen whole kernel corn, thawed
3 ounces smoked ham, diced into ¼-inch cubes

1. Preheat the oven to 350°F.
2. In a 4-quart saucepan, melt the butter over low heat. Stir in the flour and garlic powder until well blended, then add the milk all at once.

3. Cook the mixture over medium heat, stirring constantly to prevent scorching, until thickened and bubbly. Stir in the cream cheese and cheese sauce. Continue cooking until the cream cheese is melted, 5 to 8 minutes.
4. Stir in the corn and ham. Transfer the mixture to a 2-quart casserole dish.
5. Place the casserole dish in the oven and bake for 45 minutes, or until the top appears set with some light browning around the edges. Let rest for 5 minutes and serve.

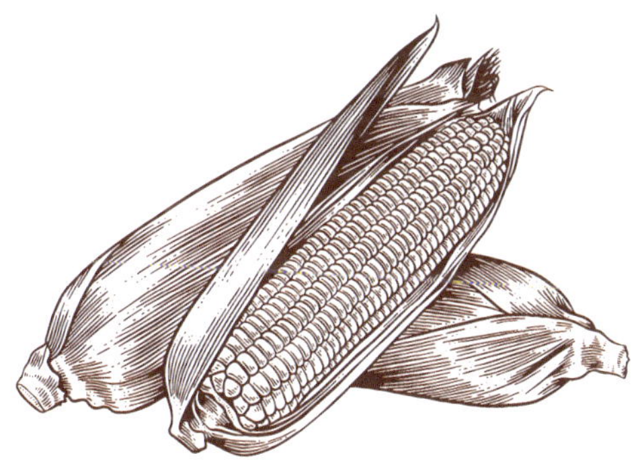

KC-STYLE BBQ BEANS

ARDIE A. DAVIS, A.K.A. REMUS POWERS, PHB

SERVES 6 TO 8

An easy, delicious, crowd-pleasing side dish that's packed with protein. This recipe took years to perfect and is based on what Chef Paul Kirk, the KC Baron of Barbecue, taught Davis about preparing barbecue beans. The bubbling pot is smoky and a little spicy—mustard is a key ingredient balancing out the sweetness of barbecue sauce and creamed corn.

3 strips thick hickory-smoked bacon*
1 medium sweet Vidalia or Texas onion, chopped
5 (15-ounce) cans pork and beans, drained and rinsed
1 (15-ounce) can creamed corn
1 (4-ounce) can chopped mild green chiles
3 cups roughly chopped barbecue brisket, burnt ends, or barbecue pork rib meat
1½ cups tomato-based barbecue sauce
⅓ cup mustard-based barbecue sauce*
Water, red wine, or beer, for thinning

** If you don't have bacon, sub ¼ cup canola oil. If you don't have a mustard-based barbecue sauce, use ⅓ cup jarred or bottled mustard.*

1. Preheat the oven or grill to 225°F. Line a plate with paper towels.
2. Place the bacon, if using, in a skillet over medium heat. Fry until crispy. Set the bacon strips aside on the plate. Reserve and transfer the bacon grease to a 5-quart Dutch oven.
3. In the Dutch oven over medium heat, sauté the onions in the bacon grease (or canola oil if substituting) for about 5 minutes, or until translucent.
4. Add the pork and beans, creamed corn, chiles, meat, and barbecue sauces. Stir for about 5 minutes, or until well combined. Add the water to thin as desired.
5. Place the Dutch oven in the preheated oven or grill. Bake or smoke the beans, uncovered, for 3 to 3½ hours, until the beans are tender and the sauce is thick and bubbling. Serve on a plate or in a ramekin.

BBQ SHRIMP

CHEF COLBY GARRELTS, CO-OWNER OF RYE

SERVES 4 TO 6

While shrimp require a bit of prep, they cook fast and hold the flavor of a rub beautifully. Here, you can cook them in a cast-iron pan on your stovetop or on a grill that's been preheated to 400°F. A little bit of heat and spice will make these a party favorite. Serve the shrimp with crusty bread or corn bread for easy-to-hold bites.

SHRIMP

2 pounds large shrimp, head-on, shell-on, and deveined

1 tablespoon smoked paprika

1 teaspoon crushed red pepper

1 teaspoon ground mustard

1 teaspoon chili powder

1 teaspoon cayenne pepper

1 teaspoon garlic powder

1 teaspoon onion powder

1 teaspoon kosher salt

1 teaspoon black pepper

2 tablespoons canola oil

SAUCE

¼ cup unsalted butter

¼ cup olive oil

6 cloves garlic, finely minced

1 small yellow onion, finely diced

½ cup Worcestershire sauce

¼ cup dark beer (such as stout)

¼ cup chicken stock

2 tablespoons dark brown sugar

1 tablespoon Rye Genuine Kansas City Hot Sauce

1 tablespoon sweet vinegar (such as champagne or apple cider vinegar)

1 tablespoon fresh thyme leaves

Juice of 1 lemon

SERVING

2 tablespoons chopped parsley, for garnish

Crusty bread or corn bread

**If you don't have Rye Genuine Kansas City Hot Sauce, opt for an equal amount of Cholula or other commercially available hot sauce.*

To make the shrimp:

1. In a large bowl, toss the shrimp with the smoked paprika, crushed red pepper, ground mustard, chili powder, cayenne pepper, garlic powder, onion powder, salt, and pepper. Let the shrimp marinate for 15 to 20 minutes while preparing the sauce.
2. Heat a large cast-iron skillet over medium-high heat. Add the canola oil and sear the shrimp in batches until just pink and lightly charred, 1 to 2 minutes per side. Remove from the skillet and set aside.

continued

To make the sauce:

1. Lower the heat to medium. Add the butter and olive oil to the same skillet. Once melted, sauté the garlic and onions until fragrant and softened, 3 to 4 minutes. Stir in the Worcestershire sauce, beer, stock, brown sugar, hot sauce, and vinegar. Bring to a simmer and let the sauce reduce slightly, about 5 minutes. Add the thyme and lemon juice. Stir to combine.

2. Return the shrimp to the skillet and toss to coat them in the sauce. Let the shrimp simmer for 3 to 4 minutes, until cooked through. Adjust seasoning with additional salt, pepper, or hot sauce as desired.

3. Garnish with the parsley and serve immediately with crusty bread or corn bread.

SAUCES, RUBS, AND RIBS

KANSAS CITY-STYLE BBQ SAUCE

JONATHAN BENDER

MAKES ABOUT 2½ CUPS

This will be the sauce that many people think of when they think of Kansas City barbecue sauce. It gets its body from ketchup and molasses, some tang from apple cider vinegar, and a touch of spice from the smoked paprika and chili powder. The sauce pours thick and can be a nice way to caramelize ribs or barbecue chicken. The key ingredient may be celery seed—a common undernote in many KC barbecue sauces that rounds off some of the flavors and ties this sauce to many on restaurant tables and grocery store shelves in Kansas City.

1 (15-ounces) can crushed tomatoes
1 cup ketchup
¾ cup brown sugar
⅓ cup apple cider vinegar
½ cup molasses
2 teaspoons black pepper
2 teaspoons smoked paprika
1 teaspoon paprika
1 teaspoon chili powder
1 teaspoon garlic powder
1 teaspoon onion powder
1 teaspoon kosher salt
½ teaspoon celery seed
½ teaspoon ground mustard
½ teaspoon red pepper flakes (optional)

1. In a medium saucepan over medium heat, place all the ingredients. Whisk together. Bring the sauce to a boil, then decrease the heat to low and gently simmer.
2. Simmer for 20 to 25 minutes, until the sauce begins to thicken and drip slowly off a wooden spoon. Remove the saucepan from the heat and let the sauce cool.
3. Transfer the sauce to an airtight container and keep in the fridge for up to 2 weeks.

MAGIC KC DRY RUB

JONATHAN BENDER

MAKES ENOUGH FOR 1-2 RACKS OF RIBS

This rub is magic because it takes only a few minutes to make, uses ingredients you likely have in your pantry, and brings a bright pop of sweetness and an undercurrent of heat to your ribs or brisket. The brown sugar is a nod to molasses, while the paprika and cayenne pepper give each bite a little kick at the end. Once you've mastered this rub, try adding other spices you enjoy.

½ cup brown sugar
¼ cup paprika*
2 tablespoons kosher salt
1 tablespoon black pepper
1 teaspoon cayenne pepper
1 tablespoon onion powder*
1 tablespoon garlic powder*
1 tablespoon chili powder

** If you don't have onion or garlic powder, you could use granulated garlic or granulated onion in the same amount. If you want to adjust the heat up or down, add or subtract ½ teaspoon cayenne pepper. You could also try subbing smoked paprika for paprika to add a rich, smoky depth to your ribs.*

1. Place all the ingredients in a medium mixing bowl and stir to combine with a small whisk or fork.
2. Your rub is now ready to use. This is a dry rub. You don't need any liquid to help bind the rub to the ribs or brisket.
3. Pat your rack of ribs (baby back pork ribs are a good choice) or brisket dry with a paper towel. Then rub the spice mix onto both sides of the meat and let it rest for 15 to 30 minutes before you place the meat on the smoker. The meat will tell you how much rub you need to use. Once the rub stops sticking to the meat, you're done.
4. If you aren't smoking ribs on the day you make this rub, place it in an airtight container and store in a cool and dry place. The rub should last for 6 months. Take a piece of painter's tape and put the date on top so you know whether it's time to make a new batch.

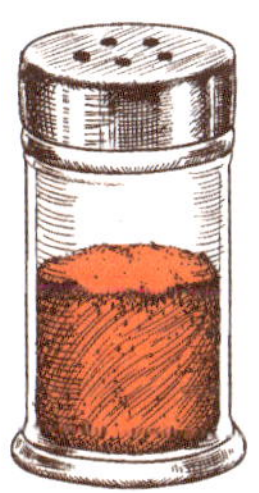

PLOWBOYS COMPETITION BBQ BABY BACK RIBS

TODD JOHNS, PITMASTER AND CO-OWNER OF PLOWBOYS BBQ

SERVES 2 TO 4

Plowboys' pork ribs garnered plenty of awards on the competition circuit. Baby back ribs come from where a pig's rib cage meets its backbone. The curved ribs are shorter than spareribs, with succulent meat from the pork loin attached at the top of the bone. Baby back ribs tend to be leaner and more tender than longer spareribs, which have a bit more fat between the bones. Here's the recipe for the succulent, tender ribs that will have you living high on the hog.

1 (3-pound) rack baby back ribs

4 ounces Plowboys BBQ Yardbird Rub*

¾ cup dark brown sugar

½ cup dark agave nectar

1 stick margarine (such as I Can't Believe It's Not Butter)

4 strips bacon (optional)

¼ teaspoon chipotle powder

½ cup Plowboys Sweet 180 BBQ sauce*

FOR YOUR SMOKER

Pecan wood chunk

Cherry wood chunks

** If you don't have Plowboys BBQ Yardbird Rub, opt for a chicken or pork rub with a little bit of sweet and heat. No Plowboys Sweet 180? Opt for a sweeter barbecue sauce with a tomato base—the Kansas City–Style BBQ Sauce recipe on page 76 would also work.*

1. Preheat your smoker to 300°F. Load the firebox with a 50/50 blend of pecan and cherry wood.
2. Using a paper towel, grip the corner of the membrane on the back of the rib. Pull to remove and discard.
3. Shake the rub liberally on both sides of the ribs. Let them sit on the counter for 20 minutes.

continued

4. Place the ribs bone side down in the smoker. Cook until the ribs take on a rich mahogany color, for 2 or 3 hours depending on the smoker.

PRO TIP 1

USE PLAIN WATER IN A SPRAY BOTTLE TO OCCASIONALLY SPRITZ THE RIBS. THIS LOWERS THE SURFACE TEMPERATURE OF THE RIBS, ALLOWING FOR MORE EVEN COOKING.

5. Lay down two sheets of aluminum foil for wrapping. Mix together the brown sugar, agave, and margarine. Rub half of the mixture on the meat side of the ribs. Lay down a bed of bacon, if using, on the foil and flip the ribs so the meat side is in contact with the bacon. Rub the other side of the ribs with the remaining mixture. Sprinkle the chipotle powder atop the ribs. Close the foil tightly and return the ribs to the smoker.

PRO TIP

SPRITZ THE BROWN SUGAR WITH WATER TO HELP IT DISSOLVE AND NOT BAKE ONTO THE RIBS.

★ ★ ★

6. After 45 minutes, open the foil to check whether the ribs are done. Don barbecue gloves. Hold two adjacent ribs and give them a twist. If they hold together, close the foil and continue cooking, checking again every 15 minutes. If the ribs begin to break apart, remove them from the smoker.
7. Fold the ends of the foil up to make a boat, careful to reserve the liquid inside. Remove the bacon, if using, and set aside to eat. With a silicone brush, apply an even layer of the barbecue sauce to thoroughly coat the back of the ribs, using the sugary liquid inside the foil to wet the brush. Flip the rack and repeat the application to the top of the ribs. Return to the smoker for 15 minutes to set the sauce.
8. Remove the ribs from the smoker. Let cool for 15 minutes. Slice to serve.

SLAP'S COMPETITION-STYLE RIBS

JOE PEARCE, CO-OWNER OF SLAP'S BBQ

SERVES 4

Tender, fall-off-the bone ribs with sweet and smoke working in harmony and a little touch of umami are what makes the lunch line go out the door at Slap's BBQ in Kansas City, Kansas. Don't expect leftovers. This recipe uses margarine, like Todd Johns's recommendation of I Can't Believe It's Not Butter, because it's easier to apply and less likely to separate at higher temperatures than butter.

- 2 racks St. Louis–style spareribs
- 2 tablespoons olive oil
- 2 teaspoons coarse sea salt or kosher salt
- 1 teaspoon black pepper
- 1 teaspoon paprika
- ½ teaspoon garlic powder
- ¼ teaspoon onion powder
- 3 ounces squeezable margarine (like Parkay)
- ¼ cup apple cider vinegar*
- ¼ cup apple juice*
- ¼ cup dark brown sugar
- 1 tablespoon Worcestershire sauce
- 1 tablespoon honey

** You can substitute cola or root beer, in equal amounts, for the apple cider vinegar and apple juice. If you like a spicier rub, add ½ teaspoon cayenne pepper or red pepper flakes.*

1. Preheat the smoker or grill to 275°F.
2. Using a paper towel, grip the corner of the membrane on the back of the rib. Pull to remove and discard.
3. In a small bowl, combine the olive oil, salt, pepper, paprika, garlic powder, and onion powder. Rub the spice mixture evenly over both sides of the ribs.
4. Smoke the ribs for 1 hour. Squeeze margarine on top of the ribs and cook for an additional hour.
5. Remove the ribs from the smoker. In a large piece of heavy-duty aluminum foil folded into a packet, combine the apple cider vinegar, apple juice, brown sugar, Worcestershire sauce, and honey. Place the ribs in the foil packet, meat side down. Seal the packet tightly. Return the ribs to the smoker and cook for 2 hours, or until the ribs reach an internal temperature of 205°F to 208°F.
6. Remove the ribs from the smoker and let rest for 10 to 15 minutes. Slice and serve.

PICNIC LUNCH AND DINNER

Q39 BRISKET

MAKES 12 TO 16

Q39 is known for its wood-finished brisket and addictive burnt ends. Brisket comes from the lower chest area of the cow. Burnt ends are usually made from the tapered edges of the brisket. The thinner edges cook faster, developing a dark, crispy bark. The crunchy exterior on the brisket surrounds a tender bite of juicy meat, which has propelled burnt ends to barbecue stardom. Beef—accented with spice and pepper—takes center stage at the Midtown restaurant forged in the fires of competitive barbecue.

1 (15- to 18-pound) certified Angus beef brisket

1 cup brisket injection*

¾ cup Q39 Brisket Rub, plus extra for dusting**

2 ounces beef stock

2 tablespoons Q39 Rib Rub, plus more for dusting**

2 cups Q39 Classic BBQ Sauce, plus more for serving**

** For the brisket injection, you can start with 1 cup beef broth or ½ cup each Minor's beef base and Minor's au jus concentrate. Feel free to add spices (black pepper, onion powder, or garlic powder) by the ½ teaspoon for additional flavor.*

*** If you don't have Q39 Brisket Rub, use a rub specifically for brisket or one with brown sugar, paprika, ancho chile powder, and chipotle. The Q39 Rib Rub has a similar spice profile with the additional kick of mustard powder. If you need a barbecue sauce substitute, look for a molasses-and-tomato-based sauce. Q39's Classic sauce gets a bit of zip from apple cider vinegar too.*

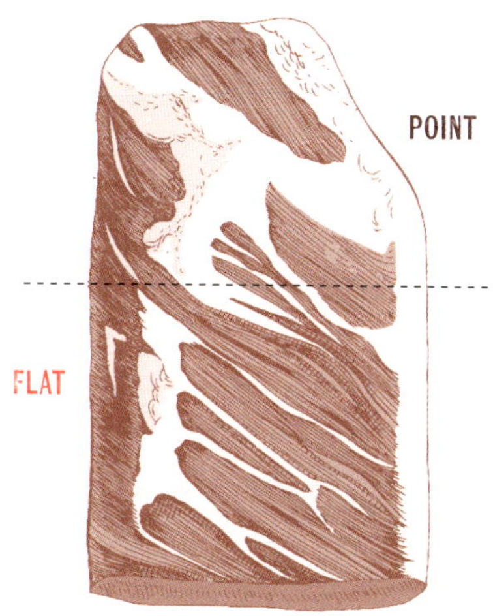

1. Trim the fat from the top of the brisket to expose the point. Leave ¼ inch of fat on the top of the flat. Trim the hard white fat from the side.

2. Place the brisket in a shallow baking dish or baking pan. Insert a meat injection syringe into the side of the brisket to add the marinade. Repeat this process six times, roughly 2 inches apart, on each side of the brisket. Wrap the brisket in plastic wrap and leave overnight in the fridge.

continued

3. Preheat the smoker to 250°F. Load the firebox with hickory wood.
4. Take the brisket out of the fridge. Unwrap it and rub an even layer of the brisket rub on all sides. Place the brisket in the smoker with the point on top. Smoke for 4 to 4½ hours, until a dark bark has formed and the internal temperature reaches 165°F.
5. Remove the brisket from the smoker. Take two sheets of heavy-duty aluminum foil—approximately 30 inches long—and wrap the brisket tightly. Add the beef stock and seal the foil pouch.
6. Place the brisket back in the smoker and cook for another 1 to 1½ hours, until the internal temperature reaches 201°F.
7. Remove the brisket from the smoker and let rest for 30 minutes. Open the foil and skim the fat off the top of the jus. Roughly 1 cup jus will remain. Reserve for later.
8. Brush the brisket with barbecue sauce and let rest for an additional 15 minutes. Place the brisket fat side down. Find the fat between the point and the flat. Use a chef's knife to separate the point from the flat, following the seam of fat (called "the nose") between the two muscles. Trim off any excess fat as you cut.

9. Fire up the grill to high. Dust the point with the rib rub and sear it for 1 minute on each side, or until the fat is rendered. Cut the point into 1-inch cubes. Toss in barbecue sauce and a dusting of rub.

10. Slice the brisket flat into ½-inch-thick slices and lay them out on a platter. Pour the reserved hot beef jus over the sliced brisket. Give it a final dusting with rub and a drizzle of barbecue sauce. Stack the burnt ends alongside the brisket slices and serve.

PORK BELLY BURNT ENDS

JONATHAN BENDER

SERVES ABOUT 10 TO 12

A delicious take on the iconic dish of Kansas City barbecue. Pork belly is subbed in for the charred crispy bits of brisket traditionally found on KC menus. The rendering of the fat in the pork belly paired with the sweet glaze makes for a delicious, rich bite.

1 (5-pound) slab pork belly, cubed into 1-inch pieces
2 tablespoons barbecue pork rub*
¼ cup sweet barbecue sauce*
24 slider buns, for serving (optional)

**Use a rub with plenty of sugar, like the Plowboys BBQ Yardbird Rub, or honey powder, like Meat Church's Honey Hog. Use a sweeter barbecue sauce with lots of brown sugar for the finishing sauce to balance out the rich, smoky pork.*

1. Preheat the smoker to 250°F. Place the pork in a bowl and toss with the rub until all sides are fully coated. Let rest for 20 to 30 minutes.
2. Place the seasoned pork fat side down on a sheet pan. Cook the pork for 3 to 3½ hours, or until it reaches an internal temperature of 195°F. Remove the sheet pan from the smoker. Place the pork and drippings into a foil pan.
3. Coat the pork with a liberal amount of barbecue sauce. Return to the smoker and cook uncovered for 1 hour, or until the pork has an internal temperature of 205°F. If the sauce is browning too quickly, cover the pan with foil. Serve with toothpicks or slider buns.

PINOT BBQ CHICKEN

JONATHAN BENDER

SERVES 6

This roasted chicken dish is a little jammy and a little smoky. The brown sugar and ketchup are a nice nod to the familiar molasses and tomato combination in many Kansas City barbecue sauces. The chicken thighs pair well with the rest of the bottle of wine, which you can also sip on while you cook.

2 tablespoons extra-virgin olive oil, plus extra for brushing
3 shallots, finely chopped
3 cloves garlic, finely chopped
1 cup ketchup
1 cup pinot noir*
2 tablespoons tightly packed light brown sugar
1 teaspoon smoked paprika
1 tablespoon Dijon mustard
½ teaspoon kosher salt
½ teaspoon black pepper
12 chicken thighs, skin-on

**If you want to cook without wine, you could substitute 1 cup pomegranate juice or ½ cup red wine vinegar and ½ cup water.*

1. In a medium saucepan, heat the olive oil over medium-low heat. After 2 minutes, add the shallots and garlic. Stir until softened, 3 to 4 minutes, lowering the heat if the ingredients start to brown.
2. Whisk in the ketchup, pinot noir, brown sugar, smoked paprika, and mustard. Bring to a boil over medium-high heat. Once boiling, bring the heat down to low and lightly simmer. Stir frequently for 15 minutes, or until the sauce thickens.
3. Let cool for 10 minutes. Use a blender or food processor to puree until smooth. Add the salt and pepper.
4. Preheat the grill to 350°F and line a plate with foil. In a large mixing bowl, lightly brush the chicken thighs with olive oil. Place the chicken skin side down on the grill top. Cook for 7 minutes. Flip and grill for an additional 7 minutes. Continue cooking, flipping and basting the chicken with the sauce every 3 minutes. Repeat at least four times (roughly 25 minutes total), until the chicken's interior temperature is 165°F. Let rest for 5 minutes on the plate and serve.

DESSERTS

SMOKED PEACH COBBLER
98

SMOKED BROWN SUGAR GINGERSNAPS
100

SMOKED PEACH COBBLER

JONATHAN BENDER

SERVES 6

The sweet peaches stand up well to smoke, and the brown sugar caramelizes in the heat for a terrific finish to a barbecue dinner. The brown sugar adds sweetness to early summer peaches, but this shines during the height of peach season. This is a terrific option in summer, a quick dessert that can cook in the smoke while you're having dinner or drinks in the backyard.

6 tablespoons unsalted butter, divided and softened
4 peaches
¼ cup dark brown sugar
1 teaspoon ground cinnamon
½ cup all-purpose flour
½ cup granulated sugar
1 teaspoon vanilla extract
½ teaspoon baking powder
½ teaspoon kosher salt
1 pint vanilla ice cream, for serving (optional)

1. Heat the smoker to 350°F. Rub a light coating using 1 tablespoon of the butter on the bottom and sides of a 9-inch cast-iron skillet.
2. Wash and slice each of the peaches into 8 slices. Leave on the skin but remove the pits. Place the peaches in a single layer in the buttered skillet. Sprinkle the brown sugar and cinnamon evenly over the top.
3. In a small mixing bowl, whisk the remaining 5 tablespoons butter together with the flour, sugar, vanilla, baking powder, and salt until well combined, or until the mixture resembles cookie dough.
4. Crumble the flour mixture on top of the peaches. Don't mix.
5. Place the skillet in the smoker and smoke for 30 to 35 minutes, until the top is golden brown and bubbly. Remove and let cool for 10 minutes before serving the cobbler on its own or over a scoop of vanilla ice cream.

SMOKED BROWN SUGAR GINGERSNAPS

JONATHAN BENDER

MAKES ABOUT 24 COOKIES

Warming spices, earthy sweetness, and a pleasing bit of smoke make these cookies an updated take on a holiday classic. These are also terrific as the two sides of an ice cream sandwich with vanilla, salted caramel, or butter pecan ice cream.

COOKIES

¼ cup tightly packed smoked brown sugar*

¾ cup tightly packed dark brown sugar

¾ cup salted butter, softened

1 egg

¼ cup molasses

1 teaspoon vanilla

2½ cups all-purpose flour

2 teaspoons ground ginger

1 teaspoon baking soda

1 teaspoon ground cinnamon

½ teaspoon nutmeg

½ teaspoon salt

SUGAR COATING

¼ cup smoked brown sugar*

¼ cup granulated sugar

½ teaspoon ground cinnamon

**You can purchase smoked brown sugar on the internet or in specialty grocers. You can also make it in your smoker without a lot of fuss.*

To make the smoked sugar:

1. Set the smoker to 160°F, or the lowest temperature setting. Add 1 cup light brown sugar to a foil pie plate or baking sheet. Mist the top lightly with water so it's wet but not dissolving.
2. Smoke the sugar for 3 to 4 hours. Stir the sugar every 45 minutes. You can give the sugar a spritz of water each time you stir to keep it from drying out.
3. Remove the sugar from the smoker and let it cool for 30 minutes. Stir it once or twice to help the heat escape. Once cool, put the sugar in an airtight container. It will keep for at least a year.

To make the cookies:

1. Preheat the oven to 350°F. Line two baking sheets with parchment paper.
2. Place the sugars and butter in a mixer. Cream for 4 to 5 minutes, until fluffy. Add the egg and beat for an additional minute until completely combined. Add the molasses and vanilla and beat on low for another minute until well combined. Scrape the sides, if necessary.

continued

3. In a large mixing bowl, place the flour, ginger, baking soda, cinnamon, nutmeg, and salt. Whisk until fully combined.
4. With the mixer on low, add the flour mixture to the creamed butter. Mix until combined, or until no white streaks of flour are visible. Stop the mixer and scrape the sides back into the dough, as necessary.
5. To make the sugar coating, add the brown sugar, granulated sugar, and cinnamon to a flat-bottomed bowl. Whisk together with a fork until the color is uniform.
6. Use a 2-tablespoon cookie scoop (or melon baller) to make dough balls (roughly ½ inch in diameter). Roll the dough balls in the sugar mixture until there's a light, even coating on the surface.
7. Place the dough balls on the baking sheets roughly 2 inches apart. Bake for 10 to 11 minutes, until the edges are firm and the middle has a slight give.
8. Remove the cookies from the oven. Let them cool on the baking sheets for 5 minutes before transferring them to a cooling rack to cool completely. Store in an airtight container for up to 1 week.

DRINKS

BLOODY BULL

ARTURO VERA-FELICIE, MIXOLOGIST

MAKES 1 COCKTAIL

A bit more full bodied and a lot more interesting than your standard Bloody Mary. The Bloody Bull is Vera-Felicie's homage to renowned mixologist Dale DeGroff's contention that savory elements can work in a cocktail. Celery bitters take the place of the standard celery stalk, while the zing of mustard creates what Vera-Felicie refers to simply as "the jam." This recipe calls for Sacramento tomato juice (tabbed by Vera-Felicie for its clean flavor profile), which is readily available online; you can also sub whatever tomato juice is at your local store.

2 dashes celery bitters
4 dashes Tabasco
1 dash fresh orange juice
1 pinch of ground black pepper
1 teaspoon whole-grain mustard
2 ounces beef stock
2 ounces vodka
2 ounces Sacramento tomato juice
Orange peel, for garnish
Whole cloves, for garnish

1. Place the bitters, Tabasco, orange juice, pepper, mustard, stock, vodka, and tomato juice in a mixing glass. Shake until well combined.
2. Serve in a tall glass over ice.
3. For the garnish, use a vegetable peeler to create a 1-inch-wide, 3-inch-long slice of orange peel. Push the pointy end of a clove into the peel, just until it sticks in the skin, about every ¼ inch. Hang the peel over the rim of the glass.

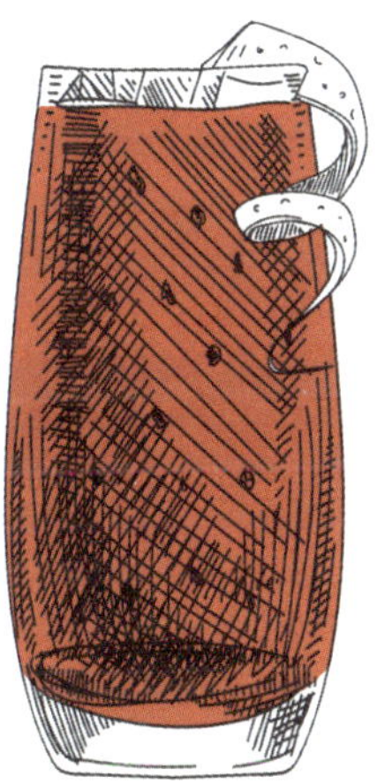

STRAWBERRY SYRUP FOR STRAWBERRY SODA

JONATHAN BENDER

MAKES ABOUT 8 TO 10 OUNCES

This strawberry syrup is light and bright—a perfect complement to the spice and smoke of barbecue. The fruit in strawberry soda is a nice balance to the mesquite flavor of brisket in Texas or paprika-laden rib rubs in Memphis. And Kansas Citians know a tall wax-coated paper cup of strawberry soda over ice is the proper way to balance the heat or pepper in barbecue sauce. This syrup is the base for freshly made strawberry soda. It's a little bit of summer in a glass with a beautiful red hue. You can also use this syrup on ice cream, pair it with whiskey in a cocktail, or add it to barbecue sauce.

SYRUP

1 cup water
Dash of lemon juice
1 cup granulated sugar

SODA

1 pint (8 to 12 ounces) strawberries, halved

To make the syrup:

1. Combine the water, lemon juice, and sugar in a medium pot. Bring to a boil over medium-high heat.
2. Add the strawberries and let the mixture return to a boil. Once it's boiling, decrease the heat to medium-low and simmer for 10 minutes.
3. Remove the pot from the stove and turn off the heat. Let the mixture cool for 2 hours.
4. Place a metal strainer over an airtight container. Pour the syrup through a strainer to remove the fruit pulp. Let it drip for 15 minutes, or gently press on the mixture with the back of a wooden spoon to get all the liquid out.
5. Refrigerate the syrup overnight before use, then store in the fridge for 1 to 2 weeks.

To make strawberry soda:

1. Combine 1 part syrup with 4 parts soda water.
2. If you're making a cocktail, use 1 ounce syrup and 2 ounces whiskey.

continued

3. If you have leftover strawberries, add 2 or 3 along with a quarter of a lemon and the syrup to a shaker tin. Muddle the ingredients with a wooden spoon handle for 5 seconds.

4. Add whiskey and ice. Put the top on the shaker tin. Shake for 10 seconds. Strain into a rocks glass over ice. Use another strawberry as a garnish.

5. The more syrup you add to the soda or cocktail, the bigger the flavor and sweetness level.

CONTRIBUTOR BIOS

JONATHAN BENDER is the founder of the Museum of BBQ. He's the author of four books, including *LEGO: A Love Story*, *Cookies & Beer*, and *Stock, Broth & Bowl*. He has judged the American Royal World Series of Barbecue, reviewed kitchen products for national publications like CNN and *Food & Wine*, and won an Emmy for a documentary about sandlot baseball. He lives in Kansas City, Missouri, with his wife and two children.

ARDIE A. DAVIS, known in the barbecue community as Remus Powers, PhB, is a 2016 Barbecue Hall of Fame inductee and a 2025 Kansas City Barbecue Society (KCBS) Hall of Fame inductee. Davis, a charter member of KCBS, founded the Diddy-Wa-Diddy National Barbecue Sauce Contest on his backyard patio in the suburbs of Roeland Park, Kansas, in 1984. The contest evolved into the American Royal Barbecue Sauce Contest in 1986 and later the American Royal World Series of Barbecue Sauce & Rub Contest. When Davis was a KCBS board member, he proposed and coauthored the KCBS Certified Barbecue Judge program and penned the Judges' Oath that is required at all KCBS-sanctioned competition barbecue contests. Davis loves to cook, eat, and judge barbecue, as well as write about it in the monthly newsletter *KC BullSheet* and *Barbecue News* magazine. He has authored or coauthored thirteen barbecue books.

ARTHUR BRYANT'S BARBEQUE was started by Charlie Bryant, who learned from the Father of Kansas City Barbecue, Henry Perry. Upon his brother's death, Arthur took over the operation and moved the restaurant to where it stands today at 18th and Brooklyn. The restaurant was near the heart of the bustling 18th and Vine District, only four blocks away from Municipal Stadium, where the Kansas City Blues and Kansas City Monarchs played. This move catapulted the restaurant to countrywide popularity. The eatery is nationally known and often recognized by experts as among the best barbecue offerings in the country. *New Yorker* writer Calvin Trillin declared that "the single best restaurant in the world is Arthur Bryant's Barbecue at 18th & Brooklyn in Kansas City."

ARTURO VERA-FELICIE was born in Puerto Rico and came to the continental United States in 1987. He joined the Marine Corps in 1999 and moved to Kansas City, Missouri, after a couple of tours overseas. He started in the service industry working the door at Buzzard Beach. He earned his first bartending award in 2009, winning the Greater Kansas City bartending competition, which is now known as the Paris of the Plains. He has spent the past decade developing bar programs for independently owned restaurants in Kansas City.

COLBY GARRELTS is a James Beard Award winner for "Best Chef Midwest" with recipes published in numerous national publications including *Bon Appétit*, *Food & Wine*, *The Wall Street Journal*, and *Saveur*. He co-owns and operates Rye with locations in Kansas City, Missouri, and Leawood, Kansas. He also leads the culinary programs at both eateries, managing kitchen teams, evolving menus, and ensuring consistency. Colby and his wife, Megan, launched Bluestem in Kansas City in 2004 and released its accompanying cookbook, *Bluestem: The Cookbook*, in 2011. Their second cookbook, *Made in America*, hit shelves in 2015.

JACK STACK BARBECUE was started in Kansas City by Russ Fiorella in 1957. Jack Stack began as a traditional storefront barbecue with a modest selection of five to six items. Jack Fiorella, the eldest son, worked with his father until 1974, when he and his wife, Delores, decided to branch off and start Fiorella's Jack Stack Barbecue in Martin City. Today, Jack Stack is in its fourth generation of family ownership.

TODD JOHNS, founder and chief pitmaster of Plowboys Barbeque, and his brother-in-law Randy Hinck started the barbecue competition team Pork Pullin Plowboys in 2001. By 2009, the team had racked up twenty-two KCBS-sanctioned competitions in seven states and five championship wins. The most sensational moment was when Plowboys returned to the American Royal Invitational and Johns was crowned the American Royal Grand Champion. Johns opened Plowboys Barbeque in Blue Springs, Missouri, in 2013, followed by two additional locations in the Kansas City metro and one in Lincoln, Nebraska. Plowboys was the official barbecue of the Kansas City Chiefs at Arrowhead Stadium for five years. Johns cohosts *BBQ Radio Network*, the most prolific syndicated barbecue show in the country.

JOE AND MIKE PEARCE are names synonymous with Kansas City barbecue. Under the team name "Squeal Like a Pig BBQ," they honed their skills on the competitive circuit, pushing the boundaries of traditional barbecue techniques. Their success on the competition circuit translated into the opening of Slap's BBQ in 2014. There, Joe and Mike brought their unique vision to life, offering a menu that blends classic Kansas City barbecue with creative twists and unexpected flavor combinations. They have appeared on national television shows like *BBQ Pitmasters*, showcasing their skills to a wider audience. Collaborations with renowned chefs like Bobby Flay and Michael Symon have further solidified their reputation as rising stars in the barbecue world. Slap's BBQ embodies the spirit of Kansas City barbecue—a tradition rooted in passion, innovation, and a relentless pursuit of flavor.

Q39 was born in barbecue competitions long before it opened. Cofounder Rob Magee won national barbecue championships and earned honors for his barbecue across the United States. Rob's journey started with a degree from the Culinary Institute of America and leading operations around the country as executive chef. Rob combined these experiences to bring a new approach to barbecue with his signature sauces and rubs. Cofounder Kelly Magee's background in business development, marketing, and technology was instrumental in making Rob's dream a reality in 2014 with the first Q39 location in Midtown Kansas City. Q39 focuses on wood-fired championship barbecue in the area's first barbecue scratch kitchen, boasting no microwaves.

METRIC CONVERSIONS

METRIC CONVERSION FORMULAS

To Convert	Multiply
Ounces to grams	Ounces by 28.35
Pounds to kilograms	Pounds by .454
Teaspoons to milliliters	Teaspoons by 4.93
Tablespoons to milliliters	Tablespoons by 14.79
Fluid ounces to milliliters	Fluid ounces by 29.57
Cups to milliliters	Cups by 240
Cups to liters	Cups by .236
Pints to liters	Pints by .473
Quarts to liters	Quarts by .946
Gallons to liters	Gallons by 3.785
Inches to centimeters	Inches by 2.54

OVEN TEMPERATURES

To convert Fahrenheit to Celsius, subtract 32 from Fahrenheit, multiply the result by 5, then divide by 9.

Description	Fahrenheit	Celsius	British Gas Mark
Very cool	200°	95°	0
Very cool	225°	110°	¼
Very cool	250°	120°	½
Cool	275°	135°	1
Cool	300°	150°	2
Warm	325°	165°	3
Moderate	350°	175°	4
Moderately hot	375°	190°	5
Fairly hot	400°	200°	6
Hot	425°	220°	7
Very hot	450°	230°	8
Very hot	475°	245°	9

APPROXIMATE METRIC EQUIVALENTS

Volume

¼ teaspoon	1 milliliter
½ teaspoon	2.5 milliliters
¾ teaspoon	4 milliliters
1 teaspoon	5 milliliters
1¼ teaspoons	6 milliliters
1½ teaspoons	7.5 milliliters
1¾ teaspoons	8.5 milliliters
2 teaspoons	10 milliliters
1 tablespoon (½ fluid ounce)	15 milliliters
2 tablespoons (1 fluid ounce)	30 milliliters
¼ cup	60 milliliters
⅓ cup	80 milliliters
½ cup (4 fluid ounces)	120 milliliters
⅔ cup	160 milliliters
¾ cup	180 milliliters
1 cup (8 fluid ounces)	240 milliliters
1¼ cups	300 milliliters
1½ cups (12 fluid ounces)	360 milliliters
1⅔ cups	400 milliliters
2 cups (1 pint)	480 milliliters
3 cups	720 milliliters
4 cups (1 quart)	0.96 liter
1 quart plus ¼ cup	1 liter
4 quarts (1 gallon)	3.8 liters

Weight

¼ ounce	7 grams
½ ounce	14 grams
¾ ounce	21 grams
1 ounce	28 grams
1¼ ounces	35 grams
1½ ounces	42.5 grams
1⅔ ounces	47 grams
2 ounces	57 grams
3 ounces	85 grams
4 ounces (¼ pound)	113 grams
5 ounces	142 grams
6 ounces	170 grams
7 ounces	198 grams
8 ounces (½ pound)	227 grams
16 ounces (1 pound)	454 grams
35.25 ounces (2.2 pounds)	1 kilogram

Length

⅛ inch	3 millimeters
¼ inch	6.25 millimeters
½ inch	1.25 centimeters
1 inch	2.5 centimeters
2 inches	5 centimeters
2½ inches	6.25 centimeters
4 inches	10 centimeters
5 inches	12.75 centimeters
6 inches	15.25 centimeters
12 inches (1 foot)	30.5 centimeters

Information compiled from a variety of sources, including *Recipes into Type* by Joan Whitman and Dolores Simon (Newton, MA: Biscuit Books, 1993); *The New Food Lover's Companion* by Sharon Tyler Herbst (Hauppauge, NY: Barron's, 2013); and *Rosemary Brown's Big Kitchen Instruction Book* (Kansas City, MO: Andrews McMeel, 1998).

THE LITTLE BOOK OF KC BBQ

The authorised representative in the EEA is Simon and Schuster Netherlands BV, Herculesplein 96 3584 AA Utrecht, Netherlands. (info@simonandschuster.nl)

Andrews McMeel Publishing
a division of Andrews McMeel Universal
1130 Walnut Street, Kansas City, Missouri 64106

www.andrewsmcmeel.com

26 27 28 29 30 TEN 10 9 8 7 6 5 4 3 2 1

ISBN: 979-8-8816-0275-8

Library of Congress Control Number: 2025942311

Editor: Jean Z. Lucas
Art Director: Holly Swayne
Production Editor: Brianna Westervelt
Production Manager: Julie Skalla

Images used under license from stock.adobe.com and shutterstock.com

KC BBQ
180